Search and Rescue Dogs

by

Charles and Linda George

Content Consultant:
Larry Peabody, Coordinator
California Rescue Dog Association

RiverFront Books

An Imprint of Franklin Watts
A Division of Grolier Publishing
New York   London   Hong Kong   Sydney
Danbury, Connecticut

RiverFront Books
http://publishing.grolier.com

Library of Congress Cataloging-in-Publication Data
George, Charles, 1949-
    Search and rescue dogs/by Charles and Linda George.
    p. cm.--(Dogs at work)
    Includes bibliographical references (p. 45) and index.
    Summary: Describes the history, selection, training, and
accomplishments of different dogs used in search and rescue operations.
    ISBN 1-56065-753-7
    1. Search dogs--Juvenile literature. 2. Rescue dogs--Juvenile literature.
[1. Search dogs. 2. Rescue dogs. 3. Search and rescue operations.] I. George,
Linda. II. Title. III. Series.
SF428.73.G46   1998
636.7'0886--dc21

                                        97-40064
                                          CIP
                                           AC

Editorial credits:
Editor, Christy Steele; cover design, James Franklin; photo research,
    Michelle L. Norstad

Photo credits:
Archive Photos, 4
Bill Faulk, cover, 16
David Macias, 7, 8, 10, 22, 24, 27, 28, 30, 32, 34, 38, 40, 43
Howard M. Paul, 13, 37
Unicorn Stock Photos/Marie Mills, 14, 19; D.F. Bunde, 20

Table of Contents

CHAPTER 1

About Search and Rescue Dogs

Dogs have been saving people's lives for hundreds of years. In the 1700s, Saint Bernards from Switzerland became the first famous search and rescue dogs. They lived with monks in the Great Saint Bernard Mountain Pass in the Alps mountains. A monk is a man who dedicates himself to serving a religious community.

Many travelers became lost while walking through the mountain pass in winter. The monks looked for lost travelers and guided people through the mountain pass. They could not do this job alone. The monks trained Saint Bernard dogs to help. Saint Bernards could find their way through blizzards or heavy fog. The dogs could find

Monks trained Saint Bernards to help them find lost travelers in the Alps.

Most search and rescue dogs wear shabracks.

people buried under snow. Saint Bernards helped the monks rescue about 2,000 travelers during the 1700s and 1800s.

In 1969, a German shepherd became the first dog in America to rescue an avalanche victim. An avalanche is a large mass of snow, ice, or earth. The mass suddenly moves down the side of a mountain. The avalanche victim was buried under seven feet (2.1 meters) of snow on Mt. Rainier in Washington state. The dog showed rescuers where the victim was buried. The rescuers dug the victim out of the snow.

Today's Search and Rescue Dogs

Today's search and rescue dogs do many things. They find people who are lost in wilderness areas. They search for people who are buried under avalanches, rockslides, or mudslides. They also search for people in buildings destroyed by bombs or earthquakes. They look for victims of plane crashes and train wrecks.

Search and rescue dogs help find people who have drowned. They find the bodies of murdered people. They also locate dead bodies after fires.

Shabracks

Most search and rescue dogs wear shabracks. A shabrack is a dog coat. Shabracks usually have a cross and the word rescue on them. Some also display the name of the dogs' search and rescue group. Shabracks let people identify search and rescue dogs.

Search and rescue dogs are most helpful in conditions that limit human senses. Dogs search well at night, in the woods, underwater, and in debris. Debris is the leftover pieces of a broken or destroyed object.

Following the Scent

For many years, search and rescue dogs were trained only for tracking or trailing. Tracking means following one person's exact path. A tracking dog follows scent trails. A scent trail is the path of smells the person leaves behind on the ground. Trailing is following one person's scent but not on the exact path the person traveled. Trailing dogs sniff the air to find the person's scent.

Tracking and trailing dogs need to smell scent articles. A scent article is an object with a person's odor on it. A scent article might be a sock, a glove, a shirt, or a pillowcase.

In the late 1960s, dog trainers Bill and Jean Syrotuck discovered that dogs could air scent. Air scenting means following all human scents

People use search and rescue dogs in bad weather and on rough ground.

Search and rescue groups are made up of volunteers.

in the air. Air scenting dogs do not need to smell scent articles. They follow any human scent present in the area they are searching. They can often cover more territory than tracking and trailing dogs. They can also search in bad weather and on rough ground. These conditions weaken the smells that tracking and trailing dogs use.

Air scenting dogs can search after long periods of time have passed. In good weather, scent stays in the air longer than it stays on the ground. Tracking and trailing dogs need to follow fresh scent trails. Otherwise the scents begin to fade.

Today, trainers teach many search and rescue dogs to track, trail, and air scent. Some dogs learn only one or two of these skills. Dogs train for one to two years before they are ready for search and rescue work.

Search and Rescue Dog Groups

In 1969, Bill and Jean Syrotuck founded the Search and Rescue Dog Association. In 1971, the Syrotucks started the American Rescue Dog Association. Other people started search and rescue dog groups, too.

Today, there are more than 150 search and rescue dog teams in North America. Search and rescue groups are made up of volunteers who own trained dogs. These groups and their dogs help people in trouble.

Each search and rescue group has its own methods of training. The groups also conduct their own tests. Dogs and their handlers need certain search and rescue skills. Both dogs and their handlers must pass tests before becoming members of a search and rescue group.

Sometimes search and rescue groups are part of local police departments. Other times, federal or state agencies contact search and rescue groups if dogs are needed. Volunteers and their dogs must be available at all times.

Volunteers usually pay for food, travel, training, and equipment expenses. The cost for most volunteers is $5,000 to $8,000 each year. Some dog food companies provide free food for the special dogs. The U.S. Air Force sometimes pays to bring dogs and their handlers to natural disasters.

Handlers

People who work with search and rescue dogs must like working with dogs. The handlers need to know their dogs' abilities and habits. Dogs and their handlers must trust each other so they can work together as teams.

Handlers should be in good physical condition. They need to be healthy enough to keep up with their dogs. Searches often cover many miles of land that contain rocks, logs, trees, or hills.

Handlers must like working with dogs.

Handlers must have certain skills. They need to know first aid. They often treat injured people until medical help arrives. It is important that handlers do not become lost. Handlers must know how to read maps and use compasses. A compass is an instrument that tells people which direction they are going.

CHAPTER 2

Best Breeds

Search and rescue dogs need certain qualities. They must be able to get along with other dogs and people. The dogs have to be willing to work. They must want to please their handlers.

Search and rescue dogs are smart. They have to learn and obey their handlers' commands. The dogs are curious about their surroundings. Fearful dogs will not be good at search and rescue work.

Search and rescue dogs must be strong. They need to work for long periods of time. The dogs learn to move quickly and easily.

Dogs from many breeds can become search and rescue dogs. Very small or very large dogs are not usually suited for search and rescue

Search and rescue dogs are curious about their surroundings.

Despite their size, Saint Bernards have special skills that allow them to work in cold, snowy conditions.

work. Large dogs cannot fit into small areas. Small dogs have short legs. It is hard for them to cover large areas.

Some breeds are better than others at searching for missing people. Saint Bernards are still used in some cold areas. Other common search and rescue breeds are bloodhounds, German shepherds, and Labrador retrievers.

Saint Bernards

Many people feel Saint Bernards are too large for search and rescue work. Saint Bernards can weigh as much as 200 pounds (90 kilograms). They may reach six feet (1.8 meters) tall when they stand on their hind legs. Their size often causes Saint Bernards to tire quickly.

But Saint Bernards have skills that make them useful despite their size. Saint Bernards work well in cold, snowy areas. They can locate people who are buried under many feet of snow. They can also sense when an avalanche is about to happen.

In Switzerland, Saint Bernards work in teams. One dog stays with the victim. This dog lies down next to the person. The dog's body heat keeps the person from freezing to death. Meanwhile, the other dog finds help.

The most famous Saint Bernard was named Barry. Barry rescued 40 people between 1800 and 1812. He retired when he was 12. Barry died of old age when he was 14.

Bloodhounds

Bloodhounds have long ears and large heads. They are 23 to 27 inches (58 to 69 centimeters) tall.

Many people consider bloodhounds best suited for trailing. This is because of their excellent sense of smell. The skin on their faces is loose and droopy. Scents are trapped in the loose folds of their skin. This helps direct smells into their noses. Bloodhounds can follow the scent trails of people lost in wilderness areas. Bloodhounds will follow scent trails until they become exhausted.

For centuries, bloodhounds have helped police track criminals. Nick Carter was one famous bloodhound. He followed more than 500 scent trails. Police caught hundreds of criminals because Nick followed scent trails to the criminals' hiding places.

German shepherds help people in many ways.

German Shepherds

German shepherds are strong, muscular dogs.
They are 22 to 26 inches (56 to 66 centimeters)
tall. They weigh 55 to 95 pounds (25 to 43
kilograms). Sometimes they work long hours
for many days in a row.

German shepherds have helped people in
many ways. During wars, the dogs carried

medicine. The dogs also guided soldiers who had been blinded in war. During peacetime, the dogs guarded families and livestock. The dogs have also helped police catch criminals.

German shepherds are the most popular dog breed for police work. This is because German shepherds are intelligent and hard working. They are curious and fearless. Strange noises or sights do not confuse them while they are searching. German shepherds bond strongly with their handlers and try to please them.

Labrador Retrievers

Labrador retrievers are muscular dogs. They are 21.5 to 24.5 inches (54.5 to 62 centimeters) tall. They weigh 55 to 70 pounds (25 to 32 kilograms).

Labrador retrievers are good at finding and retrieving objects. Their natural skill makes them good at tracking lost people.

Labrador retrievers are well-suited for swimming. Their coats protect them from cold water and bad weather.

Labrador retrievers are well suited for swimming.

CHAPTER 3

Basic Training

Most search and rescue dogs begin their training when they are several months old. Their owners help puppies get used to people. They play games with the puppies. They help puppies climb over small things. They praise the puppies often. They teach the puppies to get along with other dogs and not to bite people.

Some people train older dogs. Sometimes the older dogs have already received other kinds of training. For example, dogs might already be trained in police work or as guides for the blind.

It is important that search and rescue dogs obey their handlers' commands. Dogs learn this in obedience training. Obedience training is teaching an animal to do what it is told. Training includes learning basic commands such as sit,

It is important that search and rescue dogs obey their handlers' commands.

stay, come, and heel. Heel is a command that instructs the dog to sit at the handler's left heel.

Dogs cannot receive search and rescue training until they have passed obedience training. Then dogs are ready to learn air scenting, tracking, or trailing.

Air Scenting

Dogs trained to air scent do not usually search for one certain person. Instead, they sniff the air. They follow any human scent present in the area they are searching. Air scent dogs are used when no scent article is available. They are helpful when many people are lost. The dogs are also helpful at disaster sites where many people are trapped under debris.

Air scenting is possible because people constantly shed rafts. A raft is a dead skin cell. Rafts are shaped like tiny cereal flakes. People shed about 40,000 rafts every minute.

Each person has his or her own scent. Rafts smell like the people who shed them. Each

Dogs are helpful at disaster sites where many people are trapped under debris.

person smells different to a dog. Only identical twins may have the same scent.

People leave behind unseen clouds of rafts wherever they go. The rafts stream behind people as they walk. Search and rescue dogs sniff the air. They search for the scent of rafts. The scent becomes stronger when the dogs come closer to the missing people.

Air scent training teaches dogs to sort out scents. Handlers teach this skill by playing games with their dogs. The games are like hide and seek.

The handlers first hide and let the dogs find them. The handlers praise the dogs for finding them. Some handlers play with the dogs or give them treats.

Then another person hides with the handler. The dog finds both of them. Finally, only the other person hides. Soon, the dog learns to find people other than its handler.

Many people are usually present when dogs search for missing people. A dog goes from

Dogs search for the scent of rafts in the air.

person to person and sniffs them. Then it knows that these people are not the lost people.

Sometimes dogs make mistakes. They locate someone who is not the missing person. Dogs think a search is done if they find someone. Handlers never blame dogs for finding the wrong people. Handlers praise their dogs and send them out to search again.

Dogs pick up scent trails and follow them to find the missing people.

Tracking and Trailing

Some search and rescue dogs are better at tracking and trailing than air scenting.

Dogs are trained to follow only one scent for trailing and tracking. They learn to disregard all distractions until they have located the source of the scent.

Trailing and tracking dogs often wear chest harnesses and leashes when they work. During training, dogs learn how to move in their harnesses. They learn to work while on leashes. Leashes help handlers know where dogs are at all times. Some dogs center their attention only on the scent trails they are following. They might walk into trees or onto busy streets while following scent trails. Handlers use leashes to make sure the dogs do not hurt themselves.

During training, dogs start by following short scent trails. People hide and pretend that they are victims. The dogs are given scent articles touched by the people. The dogs smell the articles. Then the handlers command them to find the people. The dogs should pick up the scent trails and follow them to the people. The dogs are praised and rewarded when they succeed. The dogs must learn to follow longer and harder trails as training progresses.

Dogs can even follow people who are riding in cars. The people's scents blow out of car

windows. Dogs can also find and follow the scents that people leave on still water. Moving water carries the scents away.

Dogs Wearing Cameras

Sometimes dogs wear WOLVES equipment while they search. WOLVES stands for Wireless Operationally Linked Electronic and Video Exploration System.

Cameras, microphones, speakers, and receivers are part of WOLVES equipment. Cameras show when the dogs have found someone alive. Human searchers talk with trapped people by using the microphones, speakers, and receivers. A microphone is an instrument that carries sound to speakers. A speaker is a device that sends out sounds. A receiver is an instrument that receives sounds.

Dogs can find and follow the scents that people leave on still water.

CHAPTER 4

Advanced Training

Search and rescue dogs often work at disaster sites. Earthquakes, volcano eruptions, tornadoes, or bombings can create disaster sites. The dog's job is to find people trapped beneath debris.

Climbing over debris can be difficult and dangerous. The dogs must be able to balance on uneven or wet surfaces. They must not be afraid to climb over and under objects. They practice these skills during agility training.

Agility Training

Agility is the ability to move quickly and easily. Dogs travel over obstacle courses during agility training. An obstacle course is a series of barriers. A barrier is an object like a bar, fence, or wall that blocks things from

Search and rescue dogs often work at disaster sites.

going past it. Dogs must travel successfully over or through the obstacles.

Some training groups build their own obstacle courses. The groups use slides, ladders, logs, barrels, or other objects for obstacles. Dogs learn how to move slowly and carefully over or through the obstacles.

Disaster Training

Some search and rescue dogs go through disaster training. These dogs practice finding people in situations similar to those at real disaster sites. During training, people hide under rocks in old buildings. This creates a disaster-like situation.

Dogs working at disaster sites do not wear shabracks. Shabracks might get caught on debris. Then the dogs could get trapped under the debris.

Some dogs train to find people after avalanches. Trainers or handlers might hide under snow to help their dogs train. Hiding

---

Dogs learn how to handle obstacles.

under the snow can be dangerous. Only experienced trainers should do this.

Dogs continue training even after they become search and rescue dogs. They practice their search and rescue skills. This keeps their skills sharp.

Finding Dead Bodies

Sometimes people die in disasters. Search and rescue dogs may need to find these people. Victims' bodies must be taken from the debris so they can be buried properly.

Each dog reacts to finding a dead person in a different way. Each handler learns to recognize his or her dog's reaction. Some dogs back away. Others shiver and appear frightened. Some whine and beg to leave. Handlers can tell whether people are dead or alive by their dogs' reactions.

Many search and rescue dog teams went to Mexico City after the 1985 earthquake. There was so much concrete dust that handlers frequently had to clean their dogs' noses. The dogs found many dead bodies. The handlers

Only experienced trainers should hide under the snow.

stuck flags where they found dead bodies.
Workers dug out the bodies while the dogs
searched new areas.

One handler felt that the dogs needed to
experience success. The handler asked a man
to hide in the rubble. Each dog got a chance to
find the man.

CHAPTER 5

Search and Rescue Dog Stories

There are many stories about search and rescue dogs. Some dogs rescued people who were trapped under building debris. Others saved people who were buried in avalanches. Others found people who were lost in woods.

Caroline and Aly

Caroline and her German shepherd Aly searched for people after the earthquake in Mexico City. They searched the ruins of Juarez Hospital. This 12-story building caved in during the earthquake and killed at least 800 people. Some people were still alive but trapped under debris.

Aly found the scents of these people. But the danger was not over. The site was still

---

Some dogs rescued people who were trapped under building debris.

unstable. Another part of the building remained standing. It could fall if the workers moved the debris. Anyone trapped under the debris could be killed. Workers did not know whether to believe Aly.

Caroline knew Aly's habits very well. She knew Aly had found people who were alive in the debris. Caroline convinced the workers to move the debris. Workers rescued five doctors. The doctors would have died if Caroline had not trusted Aly.

Lisa and Roman

The New Mexico Search and Rescue Team helped search for a missing boy named Joseph. Joseph was hunting rabbits when he was caught in a snowstorm. No one could find him. The weather was very cold. Joseph was in danger of freezing to death.

Lisa and her German shepherd Roman searched an area that people had searched already. Roman stopped. He dropped onto his

Roman helped search for a boy lost in a snowstorm.

stomach to let Lisa know he had found Joseph. Then Roman stood up again. Joseph crawled out of the snow.

Joseph had built a shelter from sticks and snow. Then he waited under the snow for the rescuers to come. He could not get out of his shelter fast enough to signal the earlier searchers. Joseph might have frozen to death if Roman had not found him.

Rescue Dogs Help People

Search and rescue dogs save the lives of lost, hurt, or trapped people. The dogs spend most of their lives training to help in disasters.

Dogs lose some of their agility and strength as they grow old. Then handlers retire their dogs. The retired search and rescue dogs live with their handlers for the rest of their lives.

Search and rescue dogs save many people's lives.

WORDS TO KNOW

air scenting (AIR SEN-ting)—following an odor or a trail that is in the air

avalanche (AV-uh-lanch)—a large mass of snow, ice, or earth that suddenly moves down the side of a mountain

monk (MUHNGK)—a man who dedicates himself to serving a religious community.

obedience training (oh-BEE-dee-uhnss TRAY-ning)—teaching an animal to do what it is told

raft (RAFT)—a dead skin cell

scent trail (SENT TRAYL)—the path of smells a person leaves behind on the ground

tracking (TRAK-ing)—following one person's exact path

trailing (TRAY-ling)—following one person's scent but not on the exact path the person traveled

TO LEARN MORE

Curtis, Patricia. *Dogs on the Case : Search Dogs Who Help Save Lives and Enforce the Law.* New York: Lodestar Books, 1989.

Patten, Barbara. *Dogs With a Job.* Read All About Dogs Series. Vero Beach, Fla.: Rourke, 1996.

Patten, Barbara. *Hounds on the Trail.* Read All About Dogs Series. Vero Beach, Fla.: Rourke, 1996.

Ring, Elizabeth. *Search and Rescue Dogs: Expert Trackers and Trailers.* Millbrook Press, 1994.

USEFUL ADDRESSES

American Rescue Dog Association (ARDA)
P.O. Box 151
Chester, NY 10918

California Rescue Dog Association (CARDA)
9460 Vallejo Drive
Orangevale, CA 95662

National Association for Search and Rescue
4500 Southgate Place, Suite 100
Chantilly, VA 20151-1714

National Search and Rescue Secretariat
275 Slater Street
Ottawa, ON K1A 0K2
Canada

INTERNET SITES

Avalanche Dogs!
http://www.drizzle.com/~danc/avalanche.html

California Rescue Dog Association, Inc.
http://yellow.crc.ricoh.com/carda/notnetscape/
carda.html

Makor K-9 Links Page
http://www.makor-k9.com/linkpage.htm

Search and Rescue Info: SAR-Team Canine Links
http://web20.mindlink.net/sarinfo/Canine.htm

Yahoo! Internet Life: Working Dogs
http://www3.zdnet.com/yil/content/fun/animals/
wdog1.html#r2

INDEX